Honest Sonnets

Honest Sonnets

*memories from an unorthodox childhood
in verse*

by

Nicole Farmer

© 2023 Nicole Farmer. All rights reserved.
This material may not be reproduced in any form, published,
reprinted, recorded, performed, broadcast,
rewritten or redistributed without
the explicit permission of Nicole Farmer.
All such actions are strictly prohibited by law.

Cover design by Shay Culligan
Author photo by Anna Caterina

ISBN: 978-1-63980-376-7

Kelsay Books
502 South 1040 East, A-119
American Fork, Utah 84003
Kelsaybooks.com

Acknowledgements

Some of the poems in this book, or versions of them, have appeared in the following journals or magazines, which the author gratefully acknowledges.

Apricity Magazine: "Boston," "Vitamins"
The Closed Eye Open: "Mexico"
Dreamers Creative Writing: "Vitamins," "Mexico," "Boston," "Divorce"
East by Northeast Literary Review: "Theatre" (titled "19")
Kakalak: "Dyslexia"
Quillkeepers Press: "The Secret"
Sparkle and Blink, Quiet Lightening Press: "The Secret"
Viewless Wings: "Toddler, Scribe, Birthday, Daring, Conspirators"
Wingless Dreamer, My Unheard September: "Blood"
You Might Need to Hear This: "The Secret"

Thank you to Diane Suess, who was my inspiration.

I wish to give a warm thanks to my friend Kathleen Calby for her valuable edits and advice. Sincere thanks to Luke Hankins for his editing of the early poems. Much gratitude to Aaron Lelito, editor of *Wild Roof Journal,* for his advice and proofreading. Much appreciation you to Andre O. Hoilette for his Intermediate Poetry Class with Lighthouse Writer's Workshop and for the opportunity to share some of these sonnets with a small group.

Heartfelt thanks to the North Carolina Writers Network for granting me a scholarship to attend the Squire Summer Writing Workshop 2022, on the Davidson College campus, and to my instructor Jack Jung, for allowing me the time and support to focus on this project in a safe and supportive environment.

Thanks to my early readers, Carrie Tokunaga, Sonya Burres, Sarah Laliberte, and Pamela Shanks.

I also want to thank my husband and best pal, actor Mark Jeffrey Miller, who endured endless conversations and failed attempts as I tried to write about my childhood. As always, he is my first and best reader and does not fail to listen even when I wake him at four in the morning with a new idea or inspiration. (Your patience and love sustain me.)

"Snatching the eternal out of the desperately fleeting is the great magic trick of human existence."
—Tennessee Williams

*for the four of us
briefly and eternally*

Contents

Toddler	15
Heart	16
Saved	17
Legend	18
Mexico	19
Civil Rights	20
1968	21
Boston	22
Vitamins	23

*

Love	27
Greyhound	28
1969	29
What is home?	30
Chameleon	31
Idiot Box	32
England	33
Dog-Girl	34
Packing	35

*

Fire	39
Unknown	40
Gorilla Acres	41
Vegetables	42
Dyslexia	43
Scribe	44
Shoes	45
Safety	46
Notebook	47

Mr. Stewart	48
Horseplay	49
Daredevil	50
Failure	51

*

Divorce	55
Where is home?	56
Heritage	57
P.E.	58
Blood	59
Where did home go?	60

*

Birthday	63
Daring	64
Conspirators	65
High	66
Peligroso	67
Books	68
Jail	69
Crime	70

*

Education	73
Money	74
Sannyasin	75
Solo	76
Where do I make home?	77
Austin	78

Drama	79
Postcards	80
NYC	81

Appendix

Post 1	85
Post 2	86
girl meets boy	87
The Secret	89

Toddler

I was raised in a well. Scratchy wool. That smelly
tub of a rectangle, butt end of the VW bug
where I got to stand and bounce in my sandy
feet jammies, no car seat, no belts, just free
bumping along from New York City to Vermont
over every pothole or icy lump, car sickness overtaking
until I slumped into a feline coil, finger sucking
my way to slumber. World whizzing backwards,
mom smoking a joint, dad driving in a trench coat,
sister biting and pinching me in secretive battle,
blinding blizzard leaving me dizzy and excited
for more. No wonder every unexpected joy
has taken me longer to grasp, maturity late to appear.
Backwards I arrive perfectly in the rear.

Heart

Slosh and splash and twinkle your toes
flip and flop and wait to be born.
Bum-bump, bum-bump—beat of your essence.
Mana from the mama you are feeling oh so safe
you little flipper fish of an almost girl.
Twirl and kick and oh so slick it's time
to be born. Tight fight, let me exit, hey wait
this isn't so much fun, cause mom is knocked
out and can't push—forceps grab. Smack!
you're delivered with a fearsome fate
declared by the indelicate doctors—unfit,
your heart won't make it to age ten.

First glimpse at your young parents faces—
your dad's red rimmed eyes and mom biting her lip.

Saved

Not by Jesus, not by prayer, not by Satan's
underwear—just by science plain and simple,
modern medicine to the rescue! Teased in school
for the enormous bunchy scar in the shape
of a T (for Terrific, mom said) in the middle of your tiny
chest, how could they have known the trauma at three
of a giant penicillin loaded needle jabbed
daily into your bruised butt cheek, how
you'd shriek, mom by your side through the long days,
hands grasping under plastic tent flaps for months.
They didn't see you marching down the hospital hallways
with a large jar of coins on one hip, headed to the payphone
to call your dad, your rescuer, yelling loud and clear,
"Come get me outta here!"

Legend

Around our house the name Billy Burdet
was infamous, my parents telling the story
year after year. My father stood up at the rehearsal
dinner of my wedding, and was brought to tears
remembering Billy and me—this hellion I ran with
in the playroom at Boston Children's Hospital
after the surgery. Billy the kid was rushed in
when an apartment building in the projects burned down—
seventy percent of his body licked by fire's tongue,
busting bubbles and charred skin. Graft after graft
no one thought he'd make it. We found each other
right away—this crazy urchin dressed as a mummy
with the wildest laugh and a passion for playing
Fireman. Yelling, "Nee Nah, Nee Nah, Nee Nah!"

Mexico

Lemonade sandwiches, that's what we called them.
We would rumble into some little village in Mexico
in our old school bus, in the early afternoon. All
the restaurants would be closed for siesta. My sister
and I were always starving, so mom would find
a place with doors still open and we'd sit at a table
with brightly colored waxed tablecloths where
cold tortillas, limes, sugar, and condiments
remained. Mom created a meal with a tortilla,
sugar and lime juice—roll it and it's delicious!
Then it was off to pitch tents on the beach,
drink Orange Fanta or black coffee (no water,
lucky us)—no rules, hours of sun and running,
yellow streaked days changing our hair to gold.

Civil Rights

Chanting, singing, marching, forward stomping feet
ant-like perspective from a stroller—
Washington, DC, August 28th, 1963—
not my first march of shoes and legs, we hustle towards
Lincoln Memorial to hear Martin Luther King, Jr.
Me in the pram at only six months, mom pushes ahead,
her other hand grips my three-year-old sister's tiny
paw, crowds pressing in and suddenly we have lost dad.
We Shall Overcome ringing out from all sides
mom's breathing quickens, head spinning she pulls my sister
closer, reluctantly turns back to the organizer's apartment
pressing upstream against the rage of protesters.

Dad swept forward with the resolute hundreds of thousands,
"I Have a Dream" speech ricocheting off mom's back.

1968

Free love, headbands, miniskirts and protests—now
we're briefly living in an abandoned army barracks in
Westbury, Long Island—free housing for the professors.
Being Quakers, they offer some cabins to lower income
families. That's when things get interesting. Sis is seven,
I'm four, learning to defend each other in fistfights,
hair pulling/scratching brawls where we try to reclaim
stolen bikes. As a pack running through joining back
yards, we see snippets of family drama—big mamas beating
their cheating man with high heeled shoes, frying pans
thrown at heads and cussing like we've never heard,
stopping on someone's front stoop to let an older sister
plait our hair and do us up in blue eyeshadow. Lastly—dinner,
bath, and mom reading *The Chronicles of Narnia.*

Boston

They called us latchkey kids—I wore a red yarn necklace
to school each day in kindergarten, a talisman,
the tool for entry to our brownstone apartment
on display. My older sister walked me there through
busy streets and intersections while mom caught the city
bus to her secretarial job, reappearing at six o'clock—making
my way home was my own adventure. We're all separated
again—my father living in New York. I return home
first for another war with the door. A large, hungry
wooden door with all kinds of bad moods and swollen
sides that refused to budge. Yelling, begging, kicking
on the fortress for the old crone on the third floor to let me in.

Sometimes I fell asleep in the snow, waiting.
Waiting for the potion Alice drank to reach the keyhole.

Vitamins

Time went very fast like racing on a speeding train
or super slow motion like a movie reel and deathly
still—all revved up, heart pounding, I'd run around
in small circles or lie very still on the couch and hold
on to the cushions with my fists clenched and watch
the room spin. Three hours alone every day at age five is a
whopping long time. I'd make up games and sing. No
TV. Too young to read to myself. Mom was a health nut,
so no sugar in the house—only raisins. I'd stand on
the kitchen counter to reach the Fred Flintstone's—
sweet and chalky—first one, then two, then five.
Time to go visit the nosey old witch upstairs who had
Chips Ahoy! Our game was one juicy detail about my wild
hippy mom per cookie. Learning how to lie was easy.

*

Love

I grew up with this confusing twisting in my stomach.
What did the phrase *free love* mean? I couldn't figure it out.
What was happening, when dad disappeared, and mom cried?
Where did he go? Why was mom kissing our family friend
late one night when I got up for a glass of water? The seventies
were a time where what I saw adults do didn't seem free
at all, it just seemed weird. Yelling and screaming,
throwing dishes and doors slamming, cars peeling out
in the night, or hand holding and rolling in the grass on family
picnics, laughing and kissing. Up or down, high or low with no
middle ground where you knew what might be coming.

Except with us. To us they were nurturing.
Never wanting us to see the turmoil; we felt it acutely.

Greyhound

Boston to NYC every other weekend—two tiny girls.
We are seated in the front row so the driver
can see us—my mouth pressed to the window leaks
for air, eyes staring at the whizzing asphalt flying—
graffiti, trucks, cars, nothingness—parched
and bored, hoping to not have to use the latrine,
the dreaded long walk back there, loud laughing
crazies, arguments, bad smells, old men with
their hand down their pants or their thing fully
exposed trying to touch you when you walked by,
my heart racing and a green goblin in my stomach.
Dad's waiting in Port Authority, with hugs of relief.

Funny that I have no memories of what we did
on those weekends. Home was with mom, wasn't it?

1969

My parents are dancing in the fountain in Chapultepec
Park, Mexico City, joined by a bunch of students—
Arlo among them—and a dozen more college freshmen
who are enrolled in an experimental education
with my dad as their fearless leader.
We laugh and dance with the scholars never knowing
they're all high on peyote buttons or mushrooms.
We've been sleeping in an old school bus that Friends
World College bought, or on beaches, as we travel
through Mexico visiting the great ruins—Palenque,
Mitla, Monte Alban, Chechen Itza, Uxmal—dad
lectures, then sends them away to study, write their papers,
unless you're Arlo, who just writes songs. Dad'll pass him.
Half a year of non-stop surprises with melody and laughter.

What is home?

The sound of books being stacked on a shelf.
The welcoming too hot arms of my mother in the middle of the night
after another nightmare.
My sister holding my hand.

$2 + 2 = 4$

Chameleon

The story I was told was that my old man had been
on Broadway, studied with Lee Strasberg, was on
his way to being a star when he was blacklisted,
but he didn't like to talk about it, so we didn't.
He turned to academia to be a family man
but his days as a history professor proved just another stage
with students as fans—no, an entourage—
of young worshipers who believed they'd met a god.
So, when he quit with even bigger dreams to pursue, he found
himself jobless and destitute. That's when he fell
back on the skills of his youth—theft and drugs. He'd been in jail
for armed robbery at the age of eighteen, scraping his nails
in solitary. Wish I could've seen him as a Golden Gloves
boxer at fifteen, ducking and diving to save his pretty face.

Idiot Box

Feet fly over gravel, legs churn like a wagon wheel,
shale crunches underfoot. Dad holds my hand in his; on the other
side my sister struggles to keep up with his long stride. I skip.
He marches onward. What are we reading? He will always listen
if we talk about books. We are racing towards the neighbor's farm
when I see it. Right in the middle of the picture window—
the Television. A blue glow. I gasp in excitement!
My father squats before me. Just look at that box, he says.
They think they're watching IT, but it's watching THEM.
What they don't know is the more they watch
the more brain dead they become. How?
my sister asks. They stop thinking—soon they'll do whatever
it tells them to, he explained. We sigh, envious and sad for them.
We three march on into the mystery of the late summer evening.

England

Norwich, 1970: Liver on a Wednesday, fish and chips
wrapped in newspaper from a van on the corner, baked turnips,
wet bicycles, bitter winds, roses, striped bellbottoms,
umbrellas, hippies with Cockney accents—dads on a new
assignment with the college, and we followed:
my sister was sent to a private academy, with whispering,
ballet, algebra, world history, riding classes, snobbery, infighting,
and a navy-blue wool uniform with seven separate parts.
I was sent to the school "round the block with the toughs"—
street kids who hung out in the park after hours with skinheads,
knives in pockets. No uniform. While she's sipping tea
I'm with the scruffs drinking cider gripped by bloody knuckles.

We remained impenetrable in our loyalty to each other,
exchanging plots for revenge each evening before bed.

Dog-Girl

Knowing how much the British love
their dogs, I decide to become one.
I fetch sticks and retrieve them, sit pretty,
jump, lay down, stay, and bark with joy. My palms
and knees are scrapped, bloody, covered in scabs,
eventually calloused and scarred. Not only am I popular
with my school chums in Norwich, they bring treats
for "Nicky," their playground canine pal. Is this
what sociologists and anthropologists mean
when they talk about how immigrants and outsiders
assimilate? It's my fist theatre project—casting
myself as the lead, writing the script, and doing in-depth
character study! My parents were concerned about
my mental health, but I was ecstatic in my role play.

Packing

How much life fits into a cardboard box? Every year
squeezing in our treasures and new necessities
into boxes, bags, trunks, to be unpacked in some unknown
destination—house, apartment, cabin—only to leave
again, twelve to eighteen months later, to field
the same questions from strangers guessing we were military
kids and how-do-you-tell-them your dad is always restless,
driven crazy for change because greener is always somewhere
else. And you-really-wouldn't-understand. Rule Number One:
the books come first; everyone keeps their favorites. So how
was it that one move from England back to the States, mom says
our magical illustrated story book of fairytales is too
big and we must tear out the beautiful pictures, leave the words
behind? We did, but to me it felt like tearing my own flesh.

*

Fire

Burned his own house to the ground on purpose.
Backstory: Ever the sentimentalist, driving back from visiting
ex-students, radio playing John Denver—*"Almost Heaven,
West Virginia . . . country roads take me home to the place
I belong"*—dad impulsively bought a farm. We never
lived there, but once the farmhouse was only cinders
we helped to clear the land to be sold. Living up to his
city slicker upbringing with the surname Farmer for irony
he built a fire in the wood-burning stove, threw kerosine in
for good measure—the explosion threw him
to the floor, flames leaping to the curtains.
Face like a torch he runs out the back door, rolls in the grass,
drives at breakneck speed to a NY hospital, arriving home
with a mummy head, a good story and insurance money dreams.

Unknown

Awakened in darkness, a throbbing symphony of insects
in our ears, we tumble from the station wagon to face
a mammoth farmhouse. Dads got the keys, mom lays Mexican
blankets on the wooden floor of an upstairs bedroom, whispers
We're just across the hall. Tomorrow we'll explore.
Huddled together, the scratchy wool makes sleep impossible,
as moonlight stabs us through the warped windowpanes.
Then . . . THEN . . . the moaning, piercing cries that split
the dark like the snap of a giant's neck
in the jaws of a . . . What? Bear? Wolf? Wounded Lion?
How could two kids from the city know what lurked
in West Virginia's hills to torture its victims? Come
daylight the neighbor says, *Them cows been separated
from they calves 'afore market. They just bawl back and forth.*

Gorilla Acres

was what my mom named the place afterwards.
She hung a sign just beside the mailbox at the end
of the driveway, outside of Union, West Virginia. Our new
rental home was surrounded by a thousand acres of grazing land
and several hundred cows, a hillbilly paradise until a mob
of hunters descended on the old rock quarry with guns, beer
and chaw, all because a teenager had seen a "monster"
wading in the reeds the morning after he and his cronies
went to see "The Creature form the Black Lagoon." We
were told to vacate, but dad thought it would be fun to play
a joke—sitting on the front porch in a rocking chair, buck
naked, he began to jump around and act like a gorilla, scratching
his ass, as they came over the rise! Fury under my fingernails,
I went to school with the hunter's kids the next day.

Vegetables

Minutes tick to hours and still I refuse
peas, mushrooms, asparagus—gag!—so I sit
at the wooden table abandoned and alone.
Cold cruel plate locks me in its messy gaze while
the evening sings to me to come outside and play before
it's dark, voices of neighborhood kids taunt me.
*No one in the whole world has to sit here as long
as I do, with these stupid dinner rules!* I mutter.
My mom ignores me and will not bend. Then
I get smart. I hide the mess in my milk glass, (golden trick!)
in my mouth, (of course, it failed—asked to open—
she makes me swallow) tucked under a folded
fork and knife, (lame) lastly shoved in my underpants.
(Eureka! Empty it in the yard and run!)

Dyslexia

teacher at the bord standing,
row center starts with paragraf one
them, and i'm counting and sweeting
memorise my paragraphe without
turn, i'm squirming, hart beating
in front of me ascs to go to the
falling down into darkness, unable
failure, and the resounding silense
DUNCE cap placed on my

social studies book in hand, first kid, first
then the next kid back, then the next behind
dreding reading and re-reading, trying to
any flaws, it's getting closr and closer to my
too fast, trying to breathe, when the kid
bathroom, and i'm falling, falling,
to see or heer anything except my own
of turned heds, gawking to see the enormous
head

Scribe

I'm a nine-year-old writing secret messages on my mouth
with my thumbnail. Staring straight ahead at my mom,
anger like flames blowing out my ears, as I bury her
with insults written in letters that tickle my lips
and focus my rage into the written word. Our beagle sneaks
out the back door to follow the scent of a bunny,
the tracing of my finger now spelling out words
of love for my dog, my horse, my special tree, my anywhere
else but here, away from the yelling, the shit-eating
grin from my goodie-two-shoes never-get-caught
sister. In trouble again. Caught. I escape
to my hidden dialogue, stories starring me—

galloping girl who flies high, no wings needed.
Invincible and innocent in a world all my own.

Shoes

Smelled so good, brand new out of the box,
brushed suede in a patchwork of colors—
bright sunny yellow, candy apple red,
emerald green, autumn leaf brown. My mind
races at how popular these shoes will make me
at my new school. Hard to not look at them
and smile the whole way to the bus stop.
End of the day, exiting the bus, I kick them off
in the bushes, collapse in the gravel wracked by tears.
Rejected. Laughed at. Called a clown. Tripped
in the cafeteria. These kids have no idea what
fashion is, what mod means, I tell myself.

That night I rescue them, clean and display
them on my dresser like a museum installation.

Safety

The deep woods, the musky smell of fanned book pages,
each so welcoming as a place to hide that was all mine.
I first disappeared into the pages of the novel
entitled *Race Hound,* about a mistreated stray that ran away
from constant beatings and rose to fame for the speed of his gait—
Hey, just like me!—running on the wind of my imagination.
Feet like rockets, launching from the earth
to ascend the sky. My next disappearance was deep
into the snow-covered forest floor with my dog, Billy,
one December dawn, bundled in down and snow boots. We found
the perfect hide-away nestled among black oak trees and thicket—
windless and hidden—built a fire pit for heating
hot cocoa and toast. Just the two of us.
Me reading my favorite stories aloud to her twitching ears.

Notebook

In the clubhouse, only me and Suzanne were allowed.
Secrets of our fascinating lives, notes on all
our neighbors, friends, and enemies, copiously written down
in a little dark brown spiral notebook. As a fan
of Harriet the Spy, snooping and spying on everyone
was my calling. Scratching frantic notes wherever I went.
I begged for a book that was a *New York Times* bestseller in 1971,
bound to reveal mysteries of the adult world to me. *Everything You
Always Wanted to Know About Sex but Were Afraid to Ask.*
Surprisingly, dad bought it for me! I only got to read
the definitions of penis and vagina, before a 7th grade friend
of my sister stole it—the very first night I had it, hidden
under my pillow. Two weeks later she dropped out of school.
Pregnant. Bookless, we didn't understand how.

Mr. Stewart

Pink satin shirts, paisley bowtie, corduroy bellbottoms, wide belt,
blond hair falling in his eyes, full mustache—to me a god.
My fourth-grade teacher in the most unexpected
place—a small town in West Virginia. I couldn't believe
my good luck. He laughed. In homeroom he taught us
Gin Rummy, and started an all-girl softball team. When he walked,
I envisioned a runway. So, I confided my mom had been a model.
One Sunday while we were harvesting marijuana,
knee deep in green leafy buds in the kitchen, we hear a car
approaching—Panic!—and mom runs out to stall—
yelling for us to *Sweep it all into the pantry, anywhere!*
Behold his glorious self, talking with her in the driveway—he's
sashaying through our door, for tea. We sit in the pungent aroma
sipping delicately, his wide knowing smile and a wink for me.

Horseplay

Teenage turmoil turned wild competition,
we rode those horses backwards, forwards
with abandon. We invented the game, Horse Tag:
one nine-hundred-pound beast between your legs,
too little control, so much to hold as we
galloped our geldings down the hill, pell-mell,
splash dash into the pond, water spraying,
seated riders wading, now dashing about in hopes
of escaping churning hooves and reaching arms
in a game of horse and rider chase amidst riotous laughter,
giggles, whinnying and someone is calling OUT!
at the top of their lungs as a mare rolls and ditches
her soaking rider. The game begins again.
Life in the country changed our chemistry forever.

Daredevil

Midnight moonlight races in the back field,
crazy hats a must, no shoes, hair loose,
bareback mandatory, daredevil dancing,
this pack of hormone driven heartbreaks
waiting to happen, as much a herd as our lunar
intoxicated ponies, all howling and huffing
as we sped to the finish line or ended up bucked,
hurled into the thicket, maybe belly up in the hay
with the Milky Way above our pounding hearts,
dreaming of the boy who just might fall on top of you,
come to scoop you up, but no—he's off to catch
Roberta with the big boobs—and you're only thirteen,
still unseen, crazed by the summer night air,
the promise of your first kiss behind the barn.

Failure

We proved ourselves poor farmers, not living up
to the family name. My mother, a Parker, became
a glorious gardener—strong, hardworking, determined—
canning or freezing tomatoes, green beans, corn, squash,
making butter and cottage cheese, teaching us how to milk
a cow at six and at six again. Buckets sloshing with white foam,
I was in awe of her. Freedom unlike any we had ever known as
we rode our horses, adored our new family of cows, chickens,
goats, dogs, and cats. Then dad lost the farm. Busted.
Through his tears, what I saw was relief sweep his face.
He grew an excellent cash crop of marijuana, to fuel another move.
Then he lost my mom. No, she said, she'd found home. Restless
wanderer, he was off to the bayous of Louisiana. She waved
as the car pulled away. For the first time ever, we traveled
onward without her. Three again, in uncharted territory.

*

Divorce

Me and my teenage sister in the moonlight dancing
under the giant pecan tree in the back yard
high on magic shrooms for the first time, picked
from cow dung in the fields outside Lafayette,
Louisiana, dipped in honey—getting stoned with
dad, celebrating the end of the marriage, we giggle
uncontrollably, free from the troubled duo, and happy
in the knowledge they won't unite again,
ever, because six separations are enough,
and it's done! We're soaring, spiraling
across the yard with giant bobble heads, spreading
our seagull wings like our free-sailing mom.

No tears from us. Secure in their separate love.
Never again a golden foursome of dreamers and schemers.

Where is home?

The quavering voice of my sister questioning my parents.
Drowning them out, the smell of dog breath, as me and my pup both
put our noses out the window for air.

2 + 2 = 3

Heritage

He called me Nick, like a dude, like a hepcat,
same name as his Italian grandfather, the one
who came from Calabria in the 1920s, entering
through Ellis Island, ending up in Chicago, having
twelve kids with Rose Velrti. My old man asked
my opinion or what I thought about as often as he
would bark orders, taught me to clean a toilet
so sparkling that you could drink from it, took me
everywhere with him, riding sans seatbelts, shooting
the shit, laughing, cruising, irreverent and opinionated
unless of course he was pissed off, or in deep contemplation—
then I knew how to keep quiet, not contradict.

He had a temper he never unleashed on me.
I understood he had fire in his brain.

P.E.

Nightmare—not the exercise but the choosing
of teams by some popular jocks. You're the last pick.
No matter what age or which new school,
the pattern continues. By middle school I have learned
to have my folks write an excuse, or write my own—
demanding that I rest that day due to my open-heart
surgery (a truth, but not a hinderance) or my time of month
(a lie, always a lie). I am tempted to add details
like being Heart Baby of the Year in 1966
with the American Heart Association, but never do.
One crazy coach makes me run the track as punishment.
Times me. He's impressed, has me run
a fifty-yard dash and then hurdles. Wow. Look at me,
on the track team! Part of the pack and winning ribbons.

Blood

She never showed me cool dance moves, never
instructed me how to apply makeup, never whispered
who she had a crush on in my willing ears, or shared
intimacies that had to do with sex, like some sisters.
She was shy and bookish and quiet in public as a teenager
but I could confide in her and she would always listen.
She said the same words at the same time as me, falling
into peals of uncontrollable laughter. My defender
and protector against the world. She was beautiful, lithe, and tall
with long dark wavy hair and a turn-up nose I wished I had.
On Halloween she was the Blue Witch, I was the Green.
She taught me how to shoot my first tampon. Always
my barometer of the way things are and the way things should be.
Again and again, she was the anchor to my wave-tossed heart.

Where did home go?

My sister is traveling. Gone. Now I bounce between two states.

$1 + 1 = 3$

*

Birthday

Sweet sixteen under a giant moonlit crucifix
mounted in the crater of a dormant volcano filled
with tin cans somewhere close to Antigua,
Guatemala—no party dress, no dance, no teenage
boys hugging the walls, cigarettes hanging from
hungry mouths—I'm crawling on all fours
in the mud and rain, laughing with Lorenzo
the Adventurer, my wheeler-dealer smuggler
dad, while elevated Jesus looks down on us with
golden tears—the surprise at the end of our climb,
the unexpected reveal. We roll out our sleeping
bags: Pop's puking his guts out all night in penance
for eating fruit from the market. No touristy trip,
the precursor for the pivotal drug deal.

Daring

What constitutes a memory? Dad now gone
I simply remember what I remember
true or not. There were only the two of us left
at home: seeing him emerge from the bedroom
in full priest habit as Padre Lorenzo, devout
traveler between Catholic Louisiana and Catholic
Columbia, doing God's work with a friendly smile—
flamboyant Spanish and a love of Central America,
its people, its culture. You would never guess
he had plastic bags of sugar duct taped under
his pants—practice run for the big day—
me wondering if this was really happening. Now

I ponder his desperation and fear of failure—
dreading invisibility more than death.

Conspirators

I was his eyes, his judge, his confidante:
Did his pants catch when he walked, did he look
convincingly chubby? Was his belly believable? Did he
waddle like a worshiper who loved to eat?—all I
could think about was how his white plastic
collar contrasted with the black linen shirt,
how his black shoes shone, how much
cocaine would be duct taped to his body,
what they would do to him if they caught him,
would I ever see him again, would I be allowed
to visit him in the pen? But this was 1979
and he waltzed through customs with a pirouette —
shook hands, smiled, joked—his priest
a role that far surpassed his Broadway debut.

High

The disguise and tricks all worked just like he said,
the drugs smuggled into the country, never
sold from our home: but yes, I did help
cut the magic powder with baby laxative, use
the Seal-A-Meal to make packages in our kitchen.
Nine months later, with two more trips to Columbia,
he opened the Club of his dreams on the wrong side
of the tracks, a mammoth honky-tonk in an old fruit
warehouse—J.J. Cale singing "Cocaine" in a sleepy
Louisiana town where the good times rolled,
dancers spun and dipped, and every blues band
from Chicago on down south made him The Kingpin
of Lafayette Nightlife with all the fame he craved.
Once he could have been the next James Dean.

Peligroso

Mr. X is gone somewhere following his precise plan
into the bowels of South America, meeting dealers
and killers in hotel rooms, risking all to escape devastating
poverty and failure, money being the currency of success,
high on his own terrifying daring while I'm
at my grandma's house, attending high school, pretending
to know nothing, staring at my Algebra book or out
the window in a constant state of nausea and unknowing—
has he been shot in the head, left for dead roadside
in Cali? No one to confide in, tightness like a hook in my chest,
nightmares robbing slumber. He appears, victorious, like golden
Achilles, wearing a grin so wide his teeth sparkled.

Pounding him with my fists, laughing
and crying—he never included me in the plans again.

Books

Sitting in a bus station in Mexico City
reading in silence as the platform buzzes with activity—
dad's studying *The Merchant of Venice,* his favorite revenge
story, and I am savoring every word of Raskolnikov's internal
dialogue in *Crime and Punishment,* studying the criminal mind
with the prototype sharing my bench. This is the life.
My favorite moments with him were always talking
about books and ideas—our eyes popping with excitement.
The religion that Lorenzo imparted: Never be a dullard,
Never accept the status quo, find the truth,
THINK, Damn it!
Literature is the gift; knowledge is our church.
And there will never be a TV in our living room
because after *Farenheit 451,* how could you really?

Jail

Shoplifting as a teen was not my thrill pill
unlike some girls I knew who dared each other
for the prize of a sparkly trinket from Spencer's.
Arrested at fifteen at Kmart for pocketing half a pack
of colored labels (worth ninety-eight cents) all because
I was certain they would make me the straight A student
I was determined to be—yanked to the back office by security,
interrogated by the manager, then marched through the store
in handcuffs—pushed into the cruiser, fingerprinted, six hours
spent in jail, where a young cop sadistically hung my bound
hands to a hook on the wall. With only one phone call,
I knew dad wasn't home. That left my moody Italian
grandma, who made it clear she wasn't coming. Waiting . . .
waiting for dad to spring me from the bowels of hell.

Crime

Free from the jail, I was more frightened
to get into the car with dad than walk five miles home.
He wouldn't look at me. Silent, shaking, he slammed
the car door, sat behind the wheel and stared straight
through the windshield. Not a word, not a word.
I looked at the carpet under my feet, tried not to breathe
or move. He whispered, *Nick, what happened?*
When I finished, he hit the dashboard so hard
he dented it. Slowly and deliberately he said, *Nick,*
You wanna steal, steal BIG. Rob a bank or take down
a jewelry store. 'Cause those fuckers will put you away,
and there's very little I can do to help you then.

Years later my mom told me he'd done time
for armed robbery of a liquor store. At eighteen.

*

Education

After Lorenzo's first successful haul was finished
I was off to Austin to live with mom—
fun times in a tiny one-bedroom with mattresses
on the floor which doubled as couches during the day,
decorated with colorful madras covers from India,
candles, paper lanterns; all her usual artistic
flair, where hardship was funky and the place
was immaculately clean, bursting with
love and laughter. Forced to return to high school again,
my third, after traveling with dad for months,
the whole thing just seemed pointless when I knew
he was down there doing his deals, and I didn't care
about making new friends or being popular. So I quit.
Maturity was mine already, or so I imagined.

Money

Back with my balding old man, I study to ace the GED.
Working nights at the club taking cash at the door,
as a barback, a runner from the bar to the office
movin' the mula, carting the champagne, crawfish
and spicy jambalaya for Dr. John, Alan Toussaint, Albert King,
Marcia Ball, Stevie Ray Vaughn, and a slew
of local bands. Sunday mornings at home we'd get up
late, jump start with chicory coffee and day-old donuts, draw
all the blinds, lock the doors, count money on the floor
of the living room—10's, 20's, and 100's, bound into bundles—
line them up in rows. Count and re-count. Tally the profit.
Stereo blasting Rolling Stones, *Some Girls*.

Later we could be seen planting tomatoes along the back
fence, some with 50K underneath. Never trust banks.

Sannyasin

Moms on a spiritual quest. A post-divorce
journey across America in her yellow VW bug—the Lemon.
Sleeping at KOA campgrounds in a pup tent, using a gas stove,
eating from cans—fearless and free. She followed
the Bhagwan Shree Rajneesh. Several years she
wore only the colors of the sunset and a wooden bead
necklace which had a round picture of his face sealed in Lucite.
Ever the devoted student, mediating several times a day,
listening to his lectures on her clunky cassette recorder,
then traveling to the infamous Oregon compound.
They didn't love her as much as she loved them—
she had no money. After falling off the side of a mountain,
I rushed to see her at her Haight-Ashbury commune
and she still had that radiant smile, right through the pain.

Solo

Off to a college workshop I went—Bolder, Colorado,
for a summer at Naropa Institute as the youngest enrollee
taking a writing class taught by Allen Ginsberg and Ken
Kesey, a meditation class taught by a 24-year-old hunk
who fell asleep in every meeting, and acting improvisation
taught by an old hippy chick. Three female roomies
who were so hip, sharing an apartment that had a party pool
feeling all grown up at seventeen—
watching my first Kurosawa film, skinny dipping
in the lake with boys, determined to lose my virginity,
so utterly unimpressed by Chogyam Trungpa Rinpoche,
I had dad send me a Bible.

I read the unforgiving Old Testament when finding Nirvana
on my meditation pillow wasn't working.

Where do I make home?

Anywhere I can stack my books, smell their pages, and disappear.
Backwards I am searching.

$1 + 0 = 4$

Austin

Freshman: enrolled as a Theatre major
English minor, at UT, but I never had a counselor
to discuss it. Hook 'em horns, baby, but I never
went to a football game. In the classes that inspire me,
I rock, but I'm fucking up royally
dropping courses that bore me after the drop period
learning much later they transfer as F's. Oops!
Madly in love with a tall blond Italian guy from New England.
We shimmy shack up, his trust fund keeping us afloat
even though his cheap thrill is to steal
champagne and fine wines under his trench coat (so romantic).
Drama department beyond cliquish, I join a downtown
bilingual acting troupe speaking English one night and Spanish
the next, wild howling at the moon after curtain call.

Drama

I'm nineteen, naughty, nimble, a jumble of nerves and curves
and all I obviously deserve from the endless dripping
South, cicada pounding, summer, summer, breed, breed.
He's in *Sweet Bird of Youth* with me, my romance, my solo
spectacular splash into Tennessee Williams and sweet sin.
Rehearsal over, I bend and reach for a kiwi. What's this?
Funny round rambunctious mystery rolling in my ravenous
hands. *Cut it. Cut it up,* he says. I throw back my head,
laugh a gurgling giggle, then whisper, *Let's peel it.
Feel it wet in our fingers until we mash it
between our faces.* Mouths green, we're flying down
the stairs, racing to the convertible in our wanton, willing
surrender, kiwi juice sloshing in our tight tan bellies, to drive
fast, into the salacious seduction of the twilight.

Postcards

We all wrote them. Now we were apart, we found
cool art cards and would drop a line—share the euphoria
of travel, a day at the museum, or just a moment of missing
the foursome. My sister and I now scattered
in different cities. Mom wrote her loopy scrawl
of encouragement, dad his fleeting impressions
and deep contemplations. Sis wrote careful missives
with perfect printing. My mailings were often
prolific, sending a dozen at a time when my anxiety
was high—restless wanderings dominating my days
hunting for work, romance, books, new stockings. Writing
was the glue. Torn at the seams by moments of brilliance,
a burning desire to succeed—being too weird, too quirky,
intense and misunderstood. Flying paper connected us.

NYC

Eight bags, my luggage backwards and upside down
will be left revolving around and around the carrousel at JFK
with a plan to reclaim within seven days, after I have found
a pad in Manhattan—besides, I have a taxi to catch
and a city that needs to know I have ARRIVED!
Like so many hungry minds before me with big plans and bigger
dreams. This is my birthplace, and I have finally
returned home, with talent and energy to spare. The adrenaline
coursing through my veins when entering the Village
is so strong that I have to get out, right now!
And just like Mary Tyler Moore I spin and throw my beret
(*mais oui,* I was wearing one) in the air, because it is HERE,
on my own, that I have always wanted to be!
I will make my mark. But that is a story for another time.

Appendix

Post 1

A postcard from my mother, February 1993.
The card shows a close-up photograph of a white egret.

Nicole,
The swan shows you, learning to fly during crisis.
Fly, fly up, for you have now found your freedom
And it has given you great strength.
Your intelligence, the perceptive sense you show toward life
will get you through it all.
Happy Birthday!
We have had a wonderful life together.
The love and affection you showed me all through your growing up, touches me deeply.
You never said or did one unkind thing—that's sort of a miracle (even though you might have been in your bedroom fuming!).
You had a rocky start with painful heart surgery. It was awful to watch.
But you know, early on your heart showed where all your love settled . . . in your soul.

Love,
Donna

Post 2

A postcard from my father, December 2015.
The card has a black and white photo of Anthony Hopkins onstage as King Lear.

Nick,
Trying to sort one's thoughts and feelings has never been easy for me. The negativity that has choked the rational Loren back for some time now, needs a holiday. Change was always a welcome visitor in the past, of late not so much. Self-doubt I have always lived with but could move beyond it by sheer force of energy.

The familiar is both wonderful and criminally boring.

Well, anyway kiddo, this aging is just a basket of new and delicious discoveries.
I'll keep you posted,

Love,
Dad

girl meets boy

tangled and twisted details of a given situation evade my comprehension. the intricacies of my own parents' past feels like insanity.

imagine you're a waspy small town girl from upstate new york born in the 30s who's never been filled with any confidence or encouraged just because you are a girl, not worth as much as your two brothers who you practically raised because your mother was always in the hospital with one illness or another and your father is always at the shoe factory and you blossom into this stunning androgynous beauty, run away to new york city to become a model, live a glamourous life filled with parties and adoring men that you thought only existed in magazines.

imagine you're a tough Italian kid from chicago who's so good looking and full of spunk that even in your youth of constant work as a shoe shine boy, errand boy, street hustler, would be gangster, nothing can unpolish the light that shines from your eyes and instead of just looking and talking like a movie star you pursue it and end up in manhattan studying under lee strasberg with marilyn monroe in your class, then you land a role on broadway and you're on your way to being the next james dean.

    you meet this stunning, quirky, model with the prettiest smile you have ever seen
    you meet this gorgeous, smart, short italian guy with the best laugh you have ever heard

he steals your heart, and you never recover
he gives you his loyalty because he's fallen out of love already
you give him your body and mind without question

when you get pregnant, he finds the money to send you to Mexico
    to get rid
of it in some back alley because you aren't married
and that's just what people did, but only a year later you tie the
    knot
because he is the one and only absolutely and the joy and misery
    begin.

you try to leave her again and again, but you can't
your sense of loyalty says no

you try to run away after each betrayal
but no one else compares

your love, his loyalty
love futility

The Secret

Blue

The sky weeps big pelting drops on the window. Outside the brown leaps from the trees in a windswept blur. Here, inside, my mother reaches for my hand by feeling around on the bed covers as if she is blind. She cries out for me. The death grip pulls her hard, so she clings to my warmth with a Herculean strength. Her voice like a crocodile hiss. I have something to tell you I have never told anyone before. Intake of breath as I fall forward into the cerulean unknown.

Green

Her eyes so pale and deep set like a field of new clover darkened by shadows, now red rimmed and puffy. Tired of it all. She tells me she had five daughters—two she gave away, and I think this is the dementia laughing at me. Hospital walls of puke green tighten around us, and I try to correct her. No mom, It's just me and my sis, and the unwanted pregnancy before marriage. She has no patience for my interruption—the story unfolds before me like an artichoke heart.

Purple

Two alive, that's me and my sister. One long departed from a trash bin in Mexico City down some back alley in 1956—a brief life interrupted at twelve weeks. Two, she says, created for a couple who couldn't have kids. She, the ripe plumb impregnated with a turkey baster with sperm from the fertile dad, not my dad, way before the term surrogate even existed. Twice she did this. For them. For my dad, to put him through graduate school. Not for herself. Never for herself. Behind my left ear I hear something pop inside my head. Blood purple placenta five times generated.

Orange

I hide in the sanctuary of my car. The hurricane rages around me, sheets of rain littering my windshield with leaves of rust, ginger, tiger and fire. While she sleeps, I drive mindlessly down dead-end streets decorated with Halloween pumpkins. Can this be true? When I said *Oh mom that must have been so hard for you,* she said *No, no it was easy really,* in that dreamy distant way she has where she looks right through you into a world you will never know. She turned her head away and curled into a coiled oleander caterpillar.

Yellow

I'm stumbling around the aisles of Target in a daze with sunshine colored Pine Sol in my cart. I don't remember how I got here. Who can I call? Dad died six months ago. My sister is in China and it's 3 am in Tianjin. Somewhere on this planet are two women just slightly older than me, my half-sisters, walking around with no knowledge that their genetic mother is dying. Nothing makes sense. I push my cart into the sock aisle and pick out bright lemon footies for mom's tiny bird-boned feet. Parts of me, parts of you, amber tone seagull bones.

White

The sky has melted and is running down my face so that my tears no longer taste of salt. All the Goth girls want the number of my stylist. Wet and dripping I reverse out of the parking space and almost run over an old man with a walker—I scream like a punctured tire and pound the steering wheel. When I close my eyes all I see is a blistering white starburst of rage. Why didn't she tell me sooner? Will I find the courage to ask her more? Stepping into the rehabilitation center, disinfectant mixed with feces hits my nose with a slap and the floorboards feel like quicksand parting under my feet. I am falling into a milky abyss.

Black

Spinning out into space, hurtling into the great unknown, sucked into a black hole where the truth has disappeared. Mom is sleeping. With this new knowledge, thinking of my parents' marriage, the odd comments—*That Donna, you look at her sideways and she's pregnant!*—like the distortion of a fun house mirror. Small town factory girl who ran away to the Big Apple, became a successful model only to give it all up to support her man. He owed her, big time. No one to question about this dark undisclosed act of martyrdom. My heart scorched like a shrinking raisin. Three more hours and I can call my sister. Three days later she is gone. She died alone, just as she said she would. In the pitch black of midnight, she sailed away, without ever saying another word.

Donna and Loren
on their wedding day in 1957

Author's Note

Home. I have tried to define it for years now. Many of these sonnets began as short stories or prose poems. For a few years I took classes in memoir writing. I doubted my memories, cursed the fact that I only began writing after both of my parents were dead, crumpled and tore paper after paper in frustration and failure. I'd call my sister and pick her brain and soon realized we had entirely different memories of the same event. The past can be elusive.

I found the restrictions of having to tell a story in fourteen lines, in the structure of a sonnet both comforting and challenging. Something clicked, and for three months the sonnets flowed out of me on to the page at the rate of two or three per day. Some were abandoned, some reworked. I realized the poems I was writing worked better as a group. This is why publishers often chose two or three sonnets to appear together.

Thank you so much for reading. I wish to express my deep gratitude to anyone who picks up this book of poetry, and for reading poetry at all, as we need it so much in the modern world.

—Nicole

About the Author

Nicole Farmer is a teacher living in Asheville, NC. Her poems have been published in over forty magazines including *Peregrine, Kakalak, The Closed Eye Open, Poetry South, Haunted Waters Press, Wild Roof Journal,* and *Bacopa Literary Review*. Nicole was awarded the First Prize in Prose Poetry from the *Bacopa Literary Review* in 2020. Her chapbook *Wet Underbelly Wind* was published in 2022 by Finishing Line Press. In 1990 she graduated from The Juilliard School of Drama.

Her website is:
NicoleFarmerpoetry.com

www.ingramcontent.com/pod-product-compliance
Lightning Source LLC
Chambersburg PA
CBHW030909170426
43193CB00009BA/785